FULL BELLY

POEMS

Maegen McAuliffe O'Leary

The Finished Project
© 2024

ISBN 979-8-9918767-4-2

THE FINISHED PROJECT

CREATIVITY + COURAGE + COMPASSION + COMMUNICATION

Poetry for real life, in real life.

Visit TheFinishedProject.org to support living artists and women-owned, small business.

Dedication

To past me,
from present me,
on behalf of future me,
for believing in me —

I couldn't have done it without you.

Contents

FULL BELLY

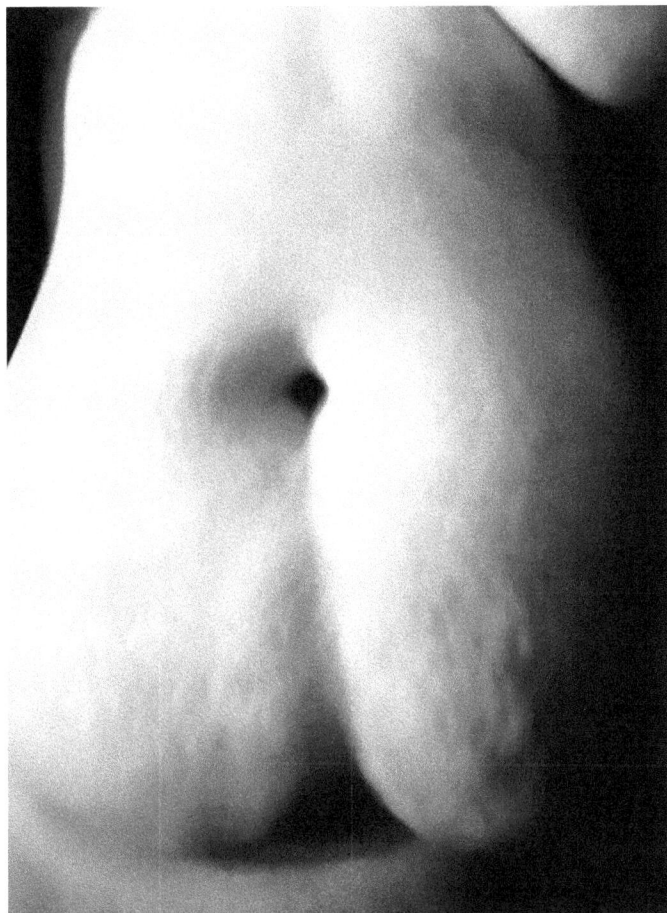

Author Self-Portrait, 20 Weeks Postpartum (2022)

Genesis

I did not create these words.
I did not carve them from wood.
I did not mold them from clay.
I did not forge them from iron.
I did not weave them from silk.

My only offering to the universe
is the swallowing whole of sorrow
and the spitting back of rage.

What I Would Tell Eve

Eat the fucking apple.
They are going to blame you
regardless.

You might as well go to the gallows
with a full belly
knowing more than God.

John 1.1-1.4

Under the chair
was the stone.

Under the stone
was the dirt.

Under the dirt
was the dead.

Under the dead
was the past.

Under the past
was the beginning.

In the beginning
was the mother.

And the mother was with God.
And the mother was God.

The same was in the beginning
with God. All things were made by her;

and without her was not any thing
made that was made. In her

was life; and the life was
the light of men.

Theophany

I. God appears

in robes and fuzzy slippers. God appears
in red lipstick half off

at the drugstore. God appears
in coffee with cream curdled cold on top

like a lifeline. God appears
in Powerball tickets.

II. God appears

while you scream into the steering wheel
after school drop off. God appears

when you least expect resistance. God appears
but you never see her. God appears

but you never see her. God appears
but you never see her. Maybe

III. you are invisible.

Sack Religious

(CALL)

Blessed are the meek
for they will inherit secrets.

Blessed are the poor
for they will inherit shame.

Blessed are the blind
for they will inherit most things.

Blessed are the weak
for they will inherit none.

(RESPONSE)

I heard they sacked Rome
and rebuilt in a day.

I heard they burn bibles
no one reads nowadays.

I won't tell a soul
but you know what they say —

blessed are the women
but you can't trust their sly ways.

Dead Line

Across it you can see
tomorrow, but you cannot touch
what is not yet here.

If you miss the boat, there is another
but they won't tell you that.
What they will say is now

do this, something, anything
before it is too late to
cross your teeth and dot your eyes.

Dead men keep mostly to themselves.
Dead women keep mostly to their thoughts
on the children.

Dead children keep mostly to their love
for tomorrow. Tomorrow
the earth will turn no longer

east to rise and west to set,
but you cannot touch
what is not yet here.

Miss Carriage

The cellular recognition of fate
presents a problem —

    to know utterly
    but control not

is to admit want for a carriage
but deny need of a horse.

Here's the Thing

There's nothing here for you. Still,
you patter about, turning over
mossyed rock, barnacled stone.

Perplexed, everything is a reminder
of the thing, but not the thing itself.
There's nothing here for you, and yet,

you build your nest from it.
You put supper on the stove.
You lay out two places.

You invite the thing home.

Cat's Cradle

Once I put a cat in a crib
and left it there while I played
across the street and of course after hours
trapped it pissed on the mattress

and my mom admonished me
for ruining the crib
but not for trapping the cat
and isn't that exactly

what's wrong with humans?
We make life a prison
and then complain
when it shits the bed.

Transition

In January I collapse

at the foot of the bed.
Origami organs fold inward
in the absence of light.
Enwombed in darkness, I
reach for myself and for a sickening
second, find only air.
I fear this

is what it means to die.
There is a sound that follows
stark despair — feral, infantile,
a driven nail. Labored breath
skipping track, retching

a song of rebirth.

How to Control Chaos

You don't. Take a breath
and wait for the end.
Keep your eyes open.

The world is magnificent
while it burns. It's good
to know how the scar forms

after the blister cracks open. It's good
to know how to form. It's good
to crack open.

The Only Way

In dreams I apologize
for things that still hurt. Forgiveness,
they say, is the only path

to absolution, and I want that.
I want to be absolved
from the stones weighting my pocket.

I want to float, face up and limbs spread
longitudinally into an impression
of the whip-soft current. All the while thinking

this is it.
This is how the body ends
and the soul begins. Loosed upon the water

and fearless of the coming breath. Knowing
I have done my part. Said sorry
to every piece of garbage that used my body

as an anchor. Confessed to weakness
of mind and hunger for madness.
Set myself drifting,

drifting,
into dissolution. The only way
out is in.

Dredging

Has its risks—fear rests
beneath loamy soil, and once
exposed to open air, oxidizes
into the mean bastard version of itself.

To alchemize pain into power, you must
uncoil tail from mouth
and allow it to rise
full height, stare cold

and steady in its wet eye,
then snatch, in one quick motion,
its pulsing throat,
and scoop, in one smooth arc,

its dangling body,
then chuck, in one cohesive loft,
its whole beasty flesh
into the waiting flame.

Cup the salubrious smoke
against center as karma curls
round your fingers
and up your nostrils

until the hard, black, tight,
little thing remaining
condenses to the period at the end
of each sentence, declaring

full stop.

The Damn Birds Are At It Again

These days, everything seems to be
a message from the other side.
Surely, this is how women lose ourselves —

open the door and start letting in
any old voice for a chat.
Surely, this is what gets us burned —

staying still too long,
listening too ferociously,
baring teeth without a smile.

For a Good Time, Call

I pursue goodness into its own
territory and seek to dominate it
with weapons of righteousness
and rage, mere womanly secrets.

The only goodness worth having
is the dead head of a benevolent mystic
who prays for the souls of lost girls.

I nail it to my bedpost
and sleep, toe in its
slack mouth, snoring.

Pythia of the Wishing Well

Warmly, with enthusiasm, I approach
the edge of the pool, where down drops

copper discs stamped with fervent meaning
and indecipherable symbols.

This, I think, will do the trick.

Give me back some level justice
or pay up the overdue fine.

The Oracle of Delphi inhales
the vapors of the earth to tell me

what I don't want to hear.

The cheese has gone sour.
The wine, turned.

Dry, the spring
that had much to say.

Dead, the god
that sought to hear it.

And I, clutching snake skin
contoured in hip and breast,

stand still, expecting miracles.

What Does My Body Tell Me

It wants? Three soft marshmallows
mashed in the cheek, a handful of cheese,
another, then another.
To rest, untouched

by God and men and children and work
emails dinging under the pillow.
The truth is I love
and I love and I love but am still

so deeply disappointed
by how ordinary this life is.
I try to sit in silent sun-washed meditation
but the scratch to know more keeps itching

and I can't reach the treetop
where the crow caws my name.
What good is silence without peace?
So I keep loving and trying and sitting

and sucking corn syrup
through my teeth, and thank Satan
he doesn't want me
but you still do.

Absolution

I am not angry anymore. I understand
holding tightly choked myself.
I know you are not malicious. I know
you are broken too. Friendship is a lie

in the face of desperate need. We would cut
saplings to beat each other
if it meant a bit of rest, a warm body, a head held
like a falling stone. I still flinch

when I hear your name.
I'm working on that. Hurt
people do much more than hurt
people, they pack grief

into a picnic basket and invite
the entire town. We were children,
all of us, and so few
given faith. Maybe

next time you offer to buy me
a drink, I still don't take it.
But I tell you hey
I wasn't thirsty

anyway. I drank
all that water
instead of letting it pass
under the bridge.

Alignment

Break me back
into some shape of a woman. I'd imagine
this fish tail comes in pretty handy

on dry land. Serpentine spine
hard to get control of; after all, how does one
tell the beginning

from the end
when my mouth is wrapped around the blunt
edge of a stick?

Luckily, I know how to swim
upstream. I know how to curve
a straight line.

Anahata

I heard the unstruck sound
inside of me. The world is on fire
and I never felt a drop

of water so cool,
heaven and earth separated
into life, before and after.

On Seeking Enlightenment

I am learning the art of detachment,
which is not the opposite of attachment,
but the cousin of resignation.

If I must, then I will,
but if I want, then I suffer,
so I accept, because I must,
and somehow, humanity will be better for it.

Somehow, I become the ant
shouldering the two-ton crumb
boulder across baked dirt

and I never stop to wipe my brow,
never consider a moment to rest,
but stoically trudge on with cake
crushing my exoskeleton

while the sun, sublimely
detached from my existence,
resigns itself to shine all day.

Wake & Bake

The point is to ricochet
from one realm to the next without stopping
in this medial plane for longer than necessary
to claim consciousness.

In case you were wondering.

I sat up on Sunday to watch the birds
go south. It's different now
but silence tastes holier
when it's smoking.

I don't mind saying so either.

Certainty cancers the soul. I keep
an eye trained on the exit. Today there is
water water everywhere
and all the trees to drink.

It's best if I stop, but don't question.

If all the smoking and gazing
lead me to ruin, still
the best dreams are the ones where I am free
of my body.

In case you were wondering.

Stock & Bond

What is there to say? Some of us
are given so much: a heart to feel and a body to hold
us, a sanctuary from our separateness.

Children to teach us divinity and a dog
to teach us compassion. The gift of saying no.
The right to take

what is ours. The openness
to know the difference. Some of us
have hands that stay filled

with gladness. Some of us
touch petals and know
the flower touches back.

Body in Motion

Here's the thing about momentum:

it starts with a push,
and then proceeds
incrementally,
at times so minute
as to appear
standing still,
and yet,
soon enough,
you're rolling downhill
with such velocity
the landscape blurs into watercolor as towns whoosh past and
bird cry streaks through your ear and
clouds trail behind in shredded ribbons and
wind whistles like a kettle at teatime and
your breath is gone before it begins and
no one can catch the force that is you
accelerating toward your future self
until you smack into it and
meld soul into body and
ask what motion was that and
how do I get

back at it again?

G.O.A.T.

Today I believe I am manifesting
the life of my dreams. I pluck
tubular daffodil stalks still wet
with dew, rabbit shit sprinkling the ground.

Yesterday I received no less than
three rejection emails, all perfunctory
politeness and ruthless indifference.
I keep a spreadsheet of my failures.

It contains no less than
one hundred and fifty-seven rows of repeated losses.
I color code the insults
by received-by date.

But fear not, this is a tale
of perseverance. Don't you know
only the great are rejected
with such voracity. I have been told no

so many times, I must be a genius
of unparalleled caliber. I must be
the goddess of refusal. I must be
the greatest of all time.

Acknowledgements

Many of these poems have appeared in varying forms on TheFinishedProject.org and on social media accounts belonging to the author and The Finished Project.

"The Damn Birds Are At It Again" was first published in Nymeria Publishing's *Descendants of Medusa Anthology* (2022).

"What I Would Tell Eve" was first published in Querencia Press's *Autumn 2022 Anthology*.

"John 1.1-1.4" contains excerpts from *King James Bible*, John 1.1-1.4.

About the Author

Maegen McAuliffe O'Leary is a poet and mother from the Pacific Northwest. Her work focuses on the contemporary human experience as it intersects feminism, matrimony, motherhood, magic, creative expression, and the human body and its place in nature. She is the author of *Bodies to Bury the Hunger* (Bottlecap Press, 2022), *Full Belly: Poems* (The Finished Project, 2024), *Richest Bastard in the Poorhouse: Poems for the Proletariat* (The Finished Project, 2025), and *Stuffed: Love Poems for Assholes* (The Finished Project, 2025).

McAuliffe O'Leary is the founder of The Finished Project, a creative communications company inspired by the sacred feminine forces of creativity, courage, compassion, and communication. The Finished Project supports living artists and women-owned, small business through an online retail platform that promotes poetry for real life, in real life. Visit TheFinishedProject.org to learn more.

*Poetry for real
life, in real life.*

.

www.ingramcontent.com/pod-product-compliance
Lightning Source LLC
Chambersburg PA
CBHW070014100426
42741CB00012B/3241